A COURSE IN

MIRACLES

CROSS

A COURSE IN
MIRACLES
CROSS

YOUR KEY TO SPIRITUAL AWAKENING

Joseph

Published by Joseph Donald De Saw II

Edited by Garnette Arledge M.Div.

ISBN E-Book: 978-1-7329246-0-4

ISBN Paperback: 978-1-7329246-1-1

The numbering of *A Course in Miracles* provides a method to
reference a specific passage within the Course and its Supplements.
Abbreviations associated with citations from the Course: T=text,
W=workbook, M=manual for teachers, C=clarification of terms.

Here is an example:
"You will first dream of peace, and then awaken to it." (T-13.VII.9:1)
T=text
13=chapter 13
VII=section VII (of chapter 13)
9=paragraph 9 (in section VII)
1=line 1 (of paragraph 9)

I thank the Foundation for Inner Peace, Inc., for the work they are
doing to make *A Course in Miracles* available to people all over the
world.

CONTENTS

INTRODUCTION

Beloved, peace be with you, all glory to God.

What follows is shared from the same spirit that inspires a pilgrim to offer refreshment to fellow travelers, as together we journey along the *way* to the *truth* of *life* eternal in the Kingdom of Heaven.

Here, in part, is what Christ Jesus says in *A Course in Miracles* (the Course) about our journey: "The journey to God is merely the reawakening of the knowledge of where you are always, and what you are forever. It is a journey without distance to a goal that has never changed" (T-8. VI.9.6).

A Course in Miracles Cross (Miracles Cross) is a key to spiritual awakening and a better understanding of three things.

First, the Miracles Cross is a key to understanding yourself—who you are, where you are, why you are here, and what you can do right now to help the world and to make your life more meaningful.

Second, the Miracles Cross is a key to understanding the teachings of *A Course in Miracles*, helping to unlock important ideas given in the Course and showing how these ideas fit together and relate to one another, making the Course easy to understand, easy to apply in daily life, and easy to share with others.

And third, the Miracles Cross is a key to understanding the Christian cross in a new way—seeing the cross as both a symbol of the ego's dream of crucifixion and death, as well as seeing the cross as a symbol showing the way to resurrection and spiritual awakening to the peace and joy of life eternal in the Kingdom of Heaven.

To describe the Miracles Cross, our narrative begins in a state of grace (the Kingdom of Heaven), followed by a fall from grace—what the Course prefers to call "the separation"—followed by reaching a turning point, and then completed by taking a path of return and reawakening to the initial state of grace.

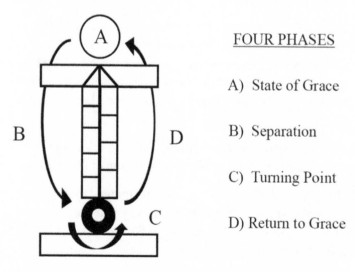

FOUR PHASES

A) State of Grace

B) Separation

C) Turning Point

D) Return to Grace

This type of circular narrative is found in a teaching story told by Jesus, known as the parable of the prodigal son (Luke

15:11–32). Noteworthy in both the parable and the teachings of *A Course in Miracles,* it is those who have freely chosen to leave the father's house, who of their own free will must decide when they have had enough of being a stranger in a strange land and, changing their mind, make the decision to return home.

The Miracles Cross is a key to help you with your journey back home and reawakening to the Kingdom of Heaven.

Please note, while this author is a Christian, there is no intent to suggest the Course or Christ Jesus or the Christian faith are the only ways of returning home and spiritual awakening. As the Course says, it is but one version of the universal curriculum. There are many teachers and forms of the universal curriculum, all leading to God in the end.

May we be led by the light of God within us all. Amen. And thank you.

CHAPTER ONE

A COURSE IN MIRACLES AND THE MEANING OF THE CROSS, CRUCIFIXION, AND RESURRECTION

A Course in Miracles is a profound, spiritual teaching in which every word has been carefully chosen and often carries a deeper meaning rather than the quick meaning we may think we know. For example, in the Course, one of the ways the word cross is used is as a noun, the name of a physical object. But another way the word *cross* is used is as a verb in the context of a journey that involves a crossing over, as in crossing over a bridge. The idea of crossing over is a central theme of the Course and used in a variety of contexts, including crossing over from perception to knowledge, from time to eternity, and from illusion to truth.

In the teachings of *A Course in Miracles,* there is an important relationship between the cross, the crucifixion, and the resurrection. In the Course, transcending, or crossing over the cross, is associated with resurrection and reawakening to life eternal in the Kingdom of Heaven. Choosing not to cross over the cross is to remain stuck, crucified to the illusions of guilt and fear, remaining asleep in a dream of separation from the peace and joy of the Kingdom of God.

Stories about the significance of crossing over can be found in all spiritual traditions. In the Bible—for example is the story of Jacob overcoming his fear and crossing over the ford at Jabbok to make peace with his brother Esau (Gen. 33:22). Another Bible story about crossing over is that of crossing the river Jordan to inherit the promised land (Josh. 3).

Similarly, the Course uses the idea of crossing over to teach that choosing to love instead of fear allows us to cross over the illusion of separation from God and claim our natural inheritance as children of God in the Kingdom of Heaven.

It is here respectfully suggested that the meaning of the Christian cross is much more than simply what may be ascribed to the crucifixion and resurrection of Jesus Christ more than two thousand years ago. The cross applies to each of us today as a symbol of our illusions, which we can choose to be crucified to, or, with help from the Holy Spirit, we can choose to cross over and be resurrected from.

For the benefit of those who may be unfamiliar with the Course, and as a refresher for those who are, below are selected excerpts from *A Course in Miracles* regarding the cross, the crucifixion, and the resurrection.

EXCERPTS FROM THE COURSE

The journey to the cross should be the last *useless journey*. Do not dwell upon it, but dismiss it as accomplished.

If you can accept it as your own last useless journey, you are also free to join my resurrection. Until you do so your life is indeed wasted. It merely re-enacts the separation, the loss of power, the futile attempts of the ego at reparation, and finally the crucifixion of the body, or death. Such repetitions are endless until they are voluntarily given up. Do not make the pathetic error of *clinging to the old rugged cross.* The only message of the crucifixion is that you can overcome the cross. Until then you are free to crucify yourself as often as you choose. This is not the gospel I intended to offer you. (T-4.in.3)

The dreary, hopeless thought that you can make attacks on others and escape yourself has nailed you to the cross. (W-196.5)

You have nailed yourself to a cross, and placed a crown of thorns upon your own head. Yet you cannot crucify God's Son, for the Will of God cannot die. His Son has been redeemed from his own crucifixion, and you cannot assign to death whom God has given eternal life. The dream of crucifixion still lies heavy on your eyes, but what you see in dreams is not reality. While you perceive the Son of God as crucified, you are asleep. And as long as you believe that you can crucify him, you are only having nightmares. You who are beginning to wake are still aware of dreams, and have not yet forgotten them. The forgetting of dreams and the awareness of Christ come with the awakening of others to share your redemption. (T-11.VI.8)

You are not really afraid of crucifixion. Your real terror is of redemption. (T-13.III.1)

A further point must be perfectly clear before any residual fear still associated with miracles can disappear. The crucifixion did not establish the Atonement; the resurrection did. Many sincere Christians have misunderstood this. No one who is free of the belief in scarcity could possibly make this mistake. If the crucifixion is seen from an upside-down point of view, it does appear as if God permitted and even encouraged one of His Sons to suffer because he was good. This particularly unfortunate interpretation, which arose out of projection, has led many people to be bitterly afraid of God. Such anti-religious concepts enter into many religions. Yet the real Christian should pause and ask, "How could this be?" Is it likely that God Himself would be capable of the kind of thinking which His Own words have clearly stated is unworthy of His Son? (T-3.I.1)

The message the crucifixion was intended to teach was that it is not necessary to perceive any form of assault in persecution, because you cannot *be* persecuted. If you respond with anger, you must be equating yourself with the destructible and are therefore regarding yourself insanely. (T-6.I.4)

The message of the crucifixion is perfectly clear:
    Teach only love, for that is what you are.
    Otherwise, I cannot serve as a model for
    learning. (T-6.I.13)

Your resurrection is your reawakening. (T-6.I.7)

The new perspective you will gain from crossing over will be the understanding of where Heaven *is*. From this side, it seems to be outside and across the bridge.

Yet as you cross to join it, it will join with you and become one with you. And you will think, in glad astonishment, that for all this you gave up *nothing*! The joy of Heaven, which has no limit, is increased with each light that returns to take its rightful place within it. (T-16.VI.11)

Sooner or later must everyone bridge the gap he imagines exists between his selves. Each one builds this bridge, which carries him across the gap as soon as he is willing to expend some little effort on behalf of bridging it. His little efforts are powerfully supplemented by the strength of Heaven, and by the united will of all who make Heaven what it is, being joined within it. And so the one who would cross over is literally transported there. (T-16.III.8)

Peace is the bridge that everyone will cross to leave this world behind. But peace begins within the world perceived as different, and leading from this fresh perception to the gate of Heaven and the way beyond. (W-200.8)

CHAPTER TWO

CIRCLE OF CREATION

The circle of creation has no end. Its starting and its ending are the same. But in itself it holds the universe of all creation, without beginning and without an end. (T-28.II.1.)

—*A Course in Miracles*

I was baptized and raised in the Roman Catholic tradition. I recall the life-size image of Jesus Christ in agony, crucified on a wooden cross, prominently displayed at the altar of our neighborhood church. And like millions of other children had been taught for more than a thousand years, I, too, was taught that if I accepted the innocent blood of Christ as the solution for washing away my sins, then when I died, I would go to Heaven. However, if I didn't accept the sacrifice of Jesus on the cross, then God would send my soul to hell to live with the devil.

When I began reading *A Course in Miracles* many years later as an adult, I noticed it spoke of a horizontal plane, a vertical axis, steps of separation, and building a ladder to heaven. In time, I was led to see how the teachings of the

A Course In Miracles Cross

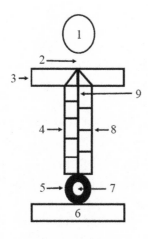

1) Circle of Creation
2) Separation
3) Longitudinal or Horizontal Plane
4) Vertical Axis Left-Hand Side
5) Dark Outer Circle
6) Foundation of Faith
7) Light Inner Circle
8) Vertical Axis Right-Hand Side
9) Arrow

Course applied to the Christian cross and how the symbol of the cross is symbolic of both a course in miracles and the teachings of *A Course in Miracles.*

The story of the Miracles Cross begins and ends with the oneness of God's all-encompassing love. I but tell you the end from the beginning.

The circle above the cross symbolizes that which lies beyond all symbols: the one true reality of God's all-encompassing love, our true home—the Kingdom of Heaven. Being Spirit, eternally limitless, this sphere of celestial order transcends the physical senses, perception teaching and learning, physics, and the laws of space and time. And while this one true reality cannot be perceived, Christ Jesus teaches in *A Course in Miracles* that this reality can be known perfectly by our reawakening to it.

Imagine a reality with nothing to fear, nothing to be upset or angry about. A reality where nothing can hurt you, where even the concept of pain does not exist. A reality with no regret or guilt for the past and no worry or anxiety regarding the future. A reality where there is only the eternal present of peace and joy in which you know you are complete and lack for nothing. A reality filled with an ever-increasing awareness of God's love for creation and creation's love for God.

In the symbolism of the Miracles Cross, this is the one true reality of which the circle above the cross reminds us.

In Christian terms, the all-encompassing circle above the cross can be understood as representing the Kingdom of God, the Kingdom of Heaven, and the eternal and infinite oneness of the Holy Trinity: God the Father, God the Son, and God the Holy Spirit.

And while the symbol of the circle exhibits attributes that lend themselves to ideas associated with the one true reality of God's all-encompassing love, such as being whole and without beginning or end, the symbol of a circle also has limitations that should be noted.

For example, someone may become so enamored with the symbol that it becomes unduly invested with value at the expense of the transcending truth beyond all symbols to which the symbol is intended to point us. Additionally, a circle has both an inner and an outer aspect. However, for purposes of the Miracles Cross, only the inner aspect of the circle above the cross has meaning, as nothing exists outside of God's all-encompassing love.

The all-encompassing, nondualistic reality of God's love is highlighted in the introduction to *A Course in Miracles*:

> The opposite of love is fear, but what is all-encompassing can have no opposite.
> This course can therefore be summed up very simply in this way:
> Nothing real can be threatened.
> Nothing unreal exists.
> Herein lies the peace of God.

For those with access to a searchable version of the Course or a concordance, suggested words to query from the Course are given at the end of this and, as applicable, subsequent chapters.

WORDS TO QUERY

circle, Creator, Father, Garden of Eden, God, Heaven, Holy Trinity, Kingdom, Knowledge, One, Sonship, State of Grace, and Truth

CHAPTER THREE

SEPARATION

A sense of separation from God is the only lack you really need correct. This sense of separation would never have arisen if you had not distorted your perception of truth, and had thus perceived yourself as lacking. (T-1.VI.2.)

—*A Course in Miracles*

The separation, gap, or empty space between the circle of creation and the horizontal plane of the Miracles Cross is symbolic of the illusion in which the children of God appear to be separated from the Kingdom of Heaven and have fallen into what the Course calls the space-time belief.

The Course teaches that the illusion of separation from the Kingdom of God began with an error, a misperception, in which part of the mind, referred to in the Course as the ego, thought it had usurped the creative power of God and used this power to create itself. The ego then judged itself as being guilty for what it believed it had done, and thinking it had committed a sin against God, the ego then became

A Course In Miracles Cross

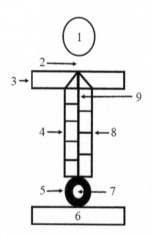

1) Circle of Creation
2) Separation
3) Longitudinal or Horizontal Plane
4) Vertical Axis Left-Hand Side
5) Dark Outer Circle
6) Foundation of Faith
7) Light Inner Circle
8) Vertical Axis Right-Hand Side
9) Arrow

fearful of God. (Please note, the word *ego* is defined differently in *A Course in Miracles* than how it is defined in Freudian psychoanalytic theories.)

In an attempt to escape from its guilt and fear, the ego proceeded down a slippery slope, ending with its imprisonment within the guilt and fear it was trying to escape from.

First, the ego tried to rid itself of its guilt and fear, the effects of its judgment, by projecting them onto God and separating itself from the Kingdom of God. But dissociation or turning away from the Kingdom of God did not rid the ego of its guilt and fear. Instead, intense anxiety was added because of the loss of contact with reality and the loss of identity with the true Self.

Second, thinking it had created itself, alone and facing a meaningless void, the ego filled its loss of reality with its own substitutions for reality, its own projections, based on its belief in guilt and fear. The big bang of the ego's projection, a twisted and distorted perception of reality, led to a condition in which illusion took the place of reality, sin took the place of guiltlessness, fear took the place of love, ego took the place of true Self, scarcity took the place of abundance, perception took the place of knowledge, madness took the place of sanity, time took the place of eternity, bondage took the place of freedom, and a dream of death took the place of eternal life.

Third, the ego then became ensnared within its illusion of guilt and fear because believing in guilt and fear is like being enslaved by a ball and chain. Throw the ball and chain of guilt and fear as far away from you as you can. Because you still believe in it, you remain connected to it. Finding yourself wherever it is you have tried to throw away the guilt and fear.

The Course teaches that because of the ego's belief in guilt and fear, the ego projects its guilt and fear outward, away from itself, as a way to try to get rid of them. However, by projecting its guilt and fear, the ego establishes for itself that guilt and fear are real, and thinking guilt and fear are real, the ego then projects its guilt and fear as a way of trying to get rid of them. And round and round it goes in a vicious cycle where A is always followed by B and B is always followed by A.

But in the dream of separation from God, an impossible situation from which there seems to be no escape, can be found the Holy Spirit of God, the Voice for God, the Universal Inspiration. More will be said about the role of the Holy Spirit later.

WORDS TO QUERY

bridge, cross over, dissociation, empty space, fear, gap, level, little space, projection, scarcity, separation, split, and substitution

EXCERPTS FROM THE COURSE REGARDING THE SEPARATION

Apart from Heaven life is illusion

There is no life outside of Heaven. Where God created life, there life must be. In any state apart from Heaven life is illusion. At best it seems like life; at worst, like death. Yet both are judgments on what is not life, equal in their inaccuracy and lack of meaning. Life not in

Heaven is impossible, and what is not in Heaven is not anywhere. Outside of Heaven, only the conflict of illusion stands; senseless, impossible and beyond all reason, and yet perceived as an eternal barrier to Heaven. Illusions are but forms. Their content is never true. (T-23.II.19)

We have discussed the fall or separation before, but its meaning must be clearly understood. The separation is a system of thought real enough in time, though not in eternity. (T-3.VII.3)

Fear

All fear is ultimately reducible to the basic misperception that you have the ability to usurp the power of God. Of course, you neither can nor have been able to do this. Here is the real basis for your escape from fear. The escape is brought about by your acceptance of the Atonement, which enables you to realize that your errors never really occurred. (T-2.I.4)

Fear produces dissociation, because it induces separation. (T-7.V.6)

Into eternity, where all is one, there crept a tiny, mad idea, at which the Son of God remembered not to laugh. (T-27.VIII.6)

On this alone the ego is correct

Recognition of meaninglessness arouses intense anxiety in all the separated ones. It represents a situation in which God and the ego "challenge" each other as to whose meaning is to be written in the empty space that meaninglessness provides. The ego rushes in frantically to establish its own ideas there, fearful that the void may otherwise be used to demonstrate its own impotence and unreality. And on this alone it is correct. (W-13.2)

Separation is maintained by projection

We have said before that the separation was and is dissociation, and that once it occurs projection becomes its main defense, or the device that keeps it going. (T-6. II.1)

The separation, split mind, ego, and Holy Spirit

The separation is merely another term for a split mind. The ego is the symbol of separation, just as the Holy Spirit is the symbol of peace. (T-5.III.9)

CHAPTER FOUR

LONGITUDINAL OR HORIZONTAL PLANE

The miracle minimizes the need for time. In the longitudinal or horizontal plane, the recognition of the equality of the members of the Sonship appears to involve almost endless time. (T-1.II.6)

—*A Course in Miracles*

In the symbolism of the Miracles Cross, one of the meanings of the cross is the illusion of space and time. The longitudinal or horizontal plane is symbolic of time, and the vertical axis is symbolic of space. In the symbolism of the Miracles Cross, the cross we bear—the burden we carry—is understood as simply the burden associated with our illusion of separation from God, which includes the illusion of space and time. But with the help of the Holy Spirit, we can learn to overcome these burdens by following the Teacher whose yoke is easy and burden light (Matt. 11:30).

Symbolically, linear time, represented by the longitudinal plane, is understood as a distortion of the circle of eternity,

A Course In Miracles Cross

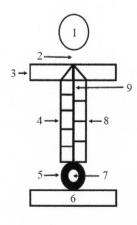

1) Circle of Creation
2) Separation
3) Longitudinal or Horizontal Plane
4) Vertical Axis Left-Hand Side
5) Dark Outer Circle
6) Foundation of Faith
7) Light Inner Circle
8) Vertical Axis Right-Hand Side
9) Arrow

without beginning or end, where the continuity of the circle appears to be broken, resulting in the circle becoming a segment with a beginning and an end.

As you face the Miracles Cross, the left-hand arm of the horizontal plane is associated with the past. The exact middle is symbolic of the present, and the right-hand arm of the cross is associated with the future.

Importantly, in addition to the cross serving as a symbol of the illusion of space and time, it serves as a symbol reminding us of God's love and the Holy Spirit. Because with us in our dream of separation from God is the Holy Spirit of God, the Universal Inspiration which has the symbolic function of reinterpreting our illusions and teaching us how to escape or awaken from these illusions. For example, regarding the ego's illusion of time and its association with loss and death, the Holy Spirit reinterprets time as a teaching device, allowing us to learn how to use time constructively for the goal of Atonement. The Course teaches that time will cease when it is no longer useful in facilitating learning (T-1.I.15.4).

We see the mediating role of the Holy Spirit symbolically expressed when Christians make the sign of the cross. God the Father is associated with the top of the vertical axis, God the Son with the bottom, and God the Holy Spirit with the longitudinal or horizontal plane mediating between the two. In the symbolism of the Miracles Cross, the mediating role of the Holy Spirit is also associated with the vertical axis right-hand side and will be discussed further in chapter 9.

WORDS TO QUERY

begin, end, future, horizon, horizontal, longitudinal, past, present, and time

EXCERPTS FROM THE COURSE REGARDING THE LONGITUDINAL OR HORIZONTAL PLANE

Space-time belief

For time and space are one illusion, which takes different forms. If it has been projected beyond your mind you think of it as time. The nearer it is brought to where it is, the more you think of it in terms of space. (T-26.VIII.1)

The Atonement was built into the space-time belief to set a limit on the need for the belief itself, and ultimately to make learning complete. (T-2.II.5)

The symbolic function of the Holy Spirit

The Holy Spirit is the only part of the Holy Trinity that has a symbolic function. He is referred to as the Healer, the Comforter and the Guide. He is also described as something "separate," apart from the Father and from the Son. I myself said, "If I go I will send you another Comforter and he will abide with you." His symbolic function makes the Holy Spirit difficult to understand, because symbolism is open to different interpretations. (T-5.I.4)

The Holy Spirit's ability to translate stumbling blocks into stepping-stones

The ego made the world as it perceives it, but the Holy Spirit, the reinterpreter of what the ego made, sees the world as a teaching device for bringing you home. (T-5.III.11)

The Holy Spirit, as always, takes what you have made and translates it into a learning device. Again as always, He reinterprets what the ego uses as an argument for separation into a demonstration against it. (T-6. V.A.2.4)

CHAPTER FIVE

VERTICAL AXIS
LEFT-HAND SIDE

The inappropriate use of extension, or projection, occurs when you believe that some emptiness or lack exists in you, and that you can fill it with your own ideas instead of truth. This process involves the following steps:

First, you believe that what God created can be changed by your own mind.

Second, you believe that what is perfect can be rendered imperfect or lacking.

Third, you believe that you can distort the creations of God, including yourself.

Fourth, you believe that you can create yourself, and that the direction of your own creation is up to you.

These related distortions represent a picture of what actually occurred in the separation, or the

A Course In Miracles Cross

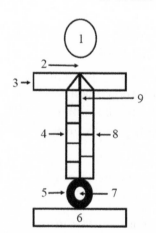

1) Circle of Creation
2) Separation
3) Longitudinal or Horizontal Plane
4) Vertical Axis Left-Hand Side
5) Dark Outer Circle
6) Foundation of Faith
7) Light Inner Circle
8) Vertical Axis Right-Hand Side
9) Arrow

"detour into fear." None of this existed before the separation, nor does it actually exist now. (T-2.I.I.)
—*A Course in Miracles*

The vertical axis of the Miracles Cross is open like a book, revealing two sides, each with a ladder and steps. As you face the Miracles Cross, the ladder on your left-hand side is symbolic of the ladder of separation described in the citation above; this is the way of the ego, downward and away from the Kingdom of Heaven. The ladder on the right-hand side is symbolic of the steps of return upon the ladder planted in the solid rock of faith and rising even to Heaven; this is the way of spiritual awakening, the way of the Holy Spirit, upward to Atonement with God and the Kingdom of Heaven.

The ladder on the left-hand side has four steps, reflecting the four steps of separation or the detour into fear described above. Because the way of the ego is downward, the steps are counted from the top down, with the first step being below the longitudinal or horizontal plane, and the fourth and final step being above the base of the vertical axis left-hand side.

More broadly, in the symbolism of the Miracles Cross, the vertical axis left-hand side is understood as symbolic of all things related to the ego, including the way of the ego, the voice of the ego, and the thought system of the ego. Again, this stands in clear contrast to the vertical axis right-hand side, which will be discussed later, and which is symbolic of the teachings of the Holy Spirit and all things the Course teaches are *right*, including right-thinking, right-choice, and right-perception.

WORDS TO QUERY

the ego

CHAPTER SIX

DARK OUTER CIRCLE

The circle of fear lies just below the level the body sees, and seems to be the whole foundation on which the world is based. Here are all the illusions, all the twisted thoughts, all the insane attacks, the fury, the vengeance, and betrayal that were made to keep the guilt in place, so that the world could rise from it and keep it hidden. Its shadow rises to the surface, enough to hold its most external manifestations in darkness, and to bring despair and loneliness to it and keep it joyless. Yet its intensity is veiled by its heavy coverings, and kept apart from what was made to keep it hidden. The body cannot see this, for the body arose from this for its protection, which depends on keeping it not seen. The body's eyes will never look on it. Yet they will see what it dictates. (T-18.IX.4.)

—*A Course in Miracles*

The four steps of separation, or the detour into fear discussed in the preceding chapter, lead to a dead end, symbolized by

A Course In Miracles Cross

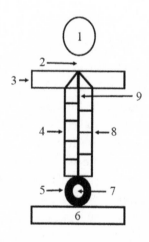

1) Circle of Creation
2) Separation
3) Longitudinal or Horizontal Plane
4) Vertical Axis Left-Hand Side
5) Dark Outer Circle
6) Foundation of Faith
7) Light Inner Circle
8) Vertical Axis Right-Hand Side
9) Arrow

the dark outer circle. Please note, the dark outer circle and the light inner circle (the doughnut or tire-like image) used in the Miracles Cross are symbolic of both darkness and light. At this stage of our survey of the Miracles Cross, the dark outer circle should be understood as being completely filled in with darkness. The light inner circle symbolic of the light of God is always there, but in the illusion of separation from God, this light is initially covered over by a veil of darkness and blocked from awareness.

Importantly, in the teachings of the Course, darkness is both nothing and the foundation or the screen upon which guilt and fear are projected giving rise to the world seen by the body's eyes. The doughnut or tire-like image used in the Miracles Cross is meant to illustrate the contrast between the outer world of darkness and the inner world of light. Spiritual awakening is a process or path of awakening from darkness to light—a process involving remembering, identifying with, and releasing the inner light. This is the path of *A Course in Miracles.*

By applying the teachings of the Course to the dark outer circle, it may be seen as symbolic of the following:

1. The foundation of a world upon which is reflected the ego's projection of guilt and fear;
2. Being egocentric and perceiving through the ego's unenlightened perspective;
3. A vicious cycle in which past guilt and fear casts a shadow, blocking awareness of the present, thus ensuring the continuation of past guilt and fear into the future;
4. And finally, as symbolic of the turning point, where one says, there must be a better way.

The dark circle is where the ego hides from God, blindly rotating in a vicious cycle of attack and defense in a chaotic universe without meaning. The dark outer circle is symbolic of the illusion of a world where fear has taken the place of love, darkness the place of light, delusions masquerade as truth, and the separated mind has made and installed the tyrant ego in place of the true Self created by our loving Father. In the Bible, Jesus says, "Take heed therefore that the light which is in thee be not darkness" (Luke 11:35).

The Course teaches that our journey home involves seeing the world the ego has made in a new light and acquiring Christ's vision, which sees the forgiven world—what the Course terms the real world. It is from the ego's world of darkness, crucifixion, and death that we are resurrected and ascend to the forgiven world of light and eternal life as we spiritually awaken and return home to "God, Whose universe is Himself" (T-11.I.2.3).

WORDS TO QUERY

circle of fear, dark, darkness, shadow, and ring of fear

EXCERPTS FROM THE COURSE REGARDING THE DARK OUTER CIRCLE

Darkness

> Darkness is lack of light as sin is lack of love. It has no unique properties of its own. It is an example of the "scarcity" belief, from which only error can proceed. (T-1.IV.3)

Made mad by guilt

The acceptance of guilt into the mind of God's Son was the beginning of the separation, as the acceptance of the Atonement is its end. The world you see is the delusional system of those made mad by guilt. Look carefully at this world, and you will realize that this is so. For this world is the symbol of punishment, and all the laws that seem to govern it are the laws of death. Children are born into it through pain and in pain. Their growth is attended by suffering, and they learn of sorrow and separation and death. Their minds seem to be trapped in their brain, and its powers to decline if their bodies are hurt. They seem to love, yet they desert and are deserted. They appear to lose what they love, perhaps the most insane belief of all. And their bodies wither and gasp and are laid in the ground, and are no more. Not one of them but has thought that God is cruel. (T-13.in.2)

If this were the real world, God *would* be cruel. For no Father could subject His children to this as the price of salvation and *be* loving. *Love does not kill to save.* If it did, attack would be salvation, and this is the ego's interpretation, not God's. Only the world of guilt could demand this, for only the guilty could conceive of it. (T-13.in.3)

This world *is* a picture of the crucifixion of God's Son. And until you realize that God's Son cannot be crucified, this is the world you will see. (T-13.in.4)

CHAPTER SEVEN

FOUNDATION OF FAITH

Faith makes the power of belief, and where it is invested determines its reward. For faith is always given what is treasured, and what is treasured is returned to you. (T-13.IX.2.)

—*A Course in Miracles*

At the top of the Miracles Cross is the circle of creation, symbolic of the system of thought founded on the truth of God's eternal and limitless love, shared by God the Father with God the Son and God the Holy Spirit. At the bottom of the Miracles Cross is the foundation of faith, symbolic of the thought system of the separated mind, which initially is based on the misperception of guilt and fear. This is the thought system that gives rise to and supports the thought system of the ego. The Course says these two systems of thought, God's and the ego's, are the only choices available to us and that every second of every minute we are choosing the one in which to place our faith.

The Course says that each of us has the responsibility and

A Course In Miracles Cross

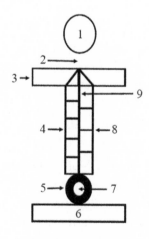

1) Circle of Creation
2) Separation
3) Longitudinal or Horizontal Plane
4) Vertical Axis Left-Hand Side
5) Dark Outer Circle
6) **Foundation of Faith**
7) Light Inner Circle
8) Vertical Axis Right-Hand Side
9) Arrow

the power to choose which of these two thought systems we want to believe in. And whether we are aware of it or not, we are always teaching the thought system we believe in to others.

The Course teaches that the thought system of the separated mind goes through three phases:

1. The first phase is associated with an unquestioned allegiance to the ego's thought system. This thought system is symbolized by the left-hand side of the vertical axis and the dark outer circle. This system of thought is based on guilt and fear and may be characterized by believing the following: "It's a dog-eat-dog world made up of winners and losers. Everyone is looking out for himself or herself, so by any means necessary, I'm going to make sure I get mine. Only might makes right. Attack me, and I will attack you back even harder." This is the thought system of those who are asleep but don't yet realize it.

2. The second phase is reaching a turning point. This occurs when the thinker becomes so bitter with the fruit of the ego's system of thought, so burdened with regret, sorrow, depression, and disease, that the thinker consciously begins to call into question the ego's thought system. Eventually the thinker becomes so sick and tired of being so sick and tired that the question is raised, "Surely there has to be a better way?" This is the thought system of those beginning to wake up.

3. And finally, the third phase is that of consciously realizing the split mind has lost its way. The thinker,

forgiving the errors made in the past, makes another choice, asking for and receiving the Holy Spirit's reinterpretation of the ego's system of thought. In time, this results in a new way of thinking—a thought system based on divine love and forgiveness, which is the undoing of the ego's system of thought. This is the thought system of those who are asleep but are now dreaming of spiritual awakening. The Course teaches that this process involves exchanging the ego's nightmare of guilt, fear, and separation for the Holy Spirit's happy dream of a forgiven world united in peace with goodwill for all.

The third phase of the split mind is symbolized by the light inner circle and the vertical axis right-hand side, which are the topics of the next two chapters.

Based on the teachings of Jesus Christ in *A Course in Miracles*, important ideas associated with the symbolism of the foundation of faith in the Miracles Cross include the following:

1. You are responsible for what you think;
2. What you think predetermines what you perceive; therefore, you are also responsible for your interpretation of what you think the eyes see;
3. There are only two thought systems to choose from; one is true and based on extending divine love and forgiveness, while the other is an error based on projecting guilt and fear;
4. Of the two thought systems, one leads straight to the Kingdom of Heaven, the other to the illusion of hell;
5. You have the power to choose which thought system you want to believe in;

6. What you think can be true or untrue;
7. What you choose to think will be true for you.

Now notice in the image of the Miracles Cross that the length of the foundation of faith is the same as the longitudinal or horizontal plane above. This symbolically expresses the idea that as long as one perceives the illusion of space and time, there is no choice but to choose which thought system in which to place one's faith: the thought system founded on love and forgiveness championed by the Holy Spirit, the Voice for God, or the thought system founded on guilt and fear, championed by the ego, which is a substitute voice made in error after dissociating or falling asleep to the reality of God's love.

Keeping these two choices in mind makes the Miracles Cross an easy tool to use in daily life. When you feel yourself to be on the wrong track consciously choose instead to be on the right track and listen to the Voice for God, accepting the eternal present within the light inner circle, which is the topic of the next chapter.

WORDS TO QUERY

belief, desire, experience, faith, foundation, mind, system of thought, thought system, and thinker

EXCERPTS FROM THE COURSE REGARDING THE FOUNDATION OF FAITH

Doing your part

> Never attempt to overlook your guilt before you ask the Holy Spirit's help. That is *His* function. Your part is

only to offer Him a little willingness to let Him remove all fear and hatred, and to be forgiven. On your little faith, joined with His understanding, He will build your part in the Atonement and make sure that you fulfill it easily. (T-18.V.2)

If you are willing to renounce the role of guardian of your thought system and open it to me, I will correct it very gently and lead you back to God. (T-4.I.4)

Responsibility for your thoughts and reaping what you sow

You may believe that you are responsible for what you do, but not for what you think. The truth is that you are responsible for what you think, because it is only at this level that you can exercise choice. What you do comes from what you think. (T-2.VI.2)

Miracles are thoughts. Thoughts can represent the lower or bodily level of experience, or the higher or spiritual level of experience. One makes the physical, and the other creates the spiritual. (T-1.I.12)

All thinking produces form at some level. (T-2.VI.9)

Once you have developed a thought system of any kind, you live by it and teach it. (T-6.in.2)

All beliefs are real to the believer. (T-3.VII.3)

Do not underestimate the power of the devotion of God's Son, nor the power the god he worships has over him. For he places himself at the altar of his god, whether it be the god he made or the God Who created him. (T-11. VI.5)

Faith and desire go hand in hand, for everyone believes in what he wants. (T-21.II.8.)

Accept sole responsibility for your ego's existence and lay aside all anger and all attack

The ego is the mind's belief that it is completely on its own. (T-4.II.8)

Do not be afraid of the ego. It depends on your mind, and as you made it by believing in it, so you can dispel it by withdrawing belief from it. Do not project the responsibility for your belief in it onto anyone else, or you will preserve the belief. When you are willing to accept sole responsibility for the ego's existence you will have laid aside all anger and all attack, because they come from an attempt to project responsibility for your own errors. But having accepted the errors as yours, do not keep them. Give them over quickly to the Holy Spirit to be undone completely, so that all their effects will vanish from your mind and from the Sonship as a whole. (*T-7. VIII.5*)

The turning point

Eventually everyone begins to recognize, however dimly, that there *must* be a better way. As this recognition becomes more firmly established, it becomes a turning point. (T-2.III.3)

Choosing is the only choice

You have chosen to be in a state of opposition in which opposites are possible. As a result, there are choices you must make. (T-5.II.6)

Each day, each hour and minute, even each second, you are deciding between the crucifixion and the resurrection; between the ego and the Holy Spirit. The ego is the choice for guilt; the Holy Spirit the choice for guiltlessness. The power of decision is all that is yours. (T-14.III.4)

The Holy Spirit and the ego are the only choices open to you. God created one, and so you cannot eradicate it. You made the other, and so you can. (T-5.V.6)

CHAPTER EIGHT

LIGHT INNER CIRCLE

The sole responsibility of the miracle worker is to accept the Atonement for himself. (T-2.V.5.)

The Atonement can only be accepted within you by releasing the inner light. (T-2.III.1.)

—*A Course in Miracles*

The light inner circle of the Miracles Cross is symbolic of the light that our Source—God the Creator, our Father—shares freely and equally with all. It is the light of divine love, the light of Spirit, the light of understanding, and the light of the eternal present free from the shadows of past guilt and fear. It is the light that gives sight to Christ's vision, illuminating the holy instant in which the truth of guiltlessness is revealed.

In the symbolism of the Miracles Cross, the light inner circle, the circle of purity, being timeless, is understood as always having been there but was initially covered over and blocked from awareness by the world of guilt and fear, symbolized by the dark outer circle.

A Course In Miracles Cross

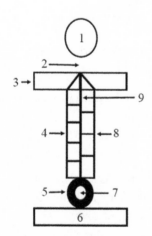

1) Circle of Creation
2) Separation
3) Longitudinal or Horizontal Plane
4) Vertical Axis Left-Hand Side
5) Dark Outer Circle
6) Foundation of Faith
7) Light Inner Circle
8) Vertical Axis Right-Hand Side
9) Arrow

As the thinker begins to question the value of following the ego's system of thought and chooses instead to follow the way of the Holy Spirit, the dark circle of fear begins to dissipate, revealing an ever-increasing inner light, the light of God's love, our true identity and natural heritage.

Initially, one may perceive the light inner circle as an article of faith, or perhaps a tiny spark, but in time, it becomes less abstract. And regardless of how the divine inner light first comes to awareness, be it a leap of faith or a flash of revelation, it is associated with the dawning of a new day and the beginning of a new way. This new direction is characterized by sharing or extending the light of God's love and grace with everyone, without exception, in all situations. The sharing of the inner light may be seen or unseen, verbal or nonverbal, focused on a particular person, situation, event, or expanded to encompass the whole world—even the entire universe of time and space and beyond.

In the symbolic imagery of the Miracles Cross, the more the thinker remembers to hold the inner light in his or her awareness and to extend or share it without exception, the more the light inner circle will expand. In time, the dark circle, which initially blocked the inner light from awareness and then seemed to be in conflict with it, will completely disappear. The miracle worker is then able to accept the translation of the inner light into the circle of creation above the Miracles Cross. As the child of God realizes it was only an illusion, which for an unholy instant seemed to keep them separate and apart.

The light inner circle of the Miracles Cross is also symbolic of what the Course terms the circle of Atonement. It is the quiet center, the inner altar, where the miracle worker rests firmly upon the solid rock of faith, believing in the truth of our Father's love for all his children. And it is here, in the peace and quiet of the inner altar to our Father, where the miracle worker lays upon the altar of God the gift of accepting Atonement with God. And it is also here, under the guidance of the Holy Spirit, where the miracle worker participates in the work of saving the world, correcting the error of misperception, dispelling the illusion of separation, healing the separated mind, and undoing the past in the present, thus releasing the future.

The practice of releasing or extending the inner light and accepting the Atonement may initially be inconsistent, but in time this is where the miracle worker learns to spend their time—doing laundry, playing with a child, talking with others, riding the bus, or reading a book. It doesn't matter, as life becomes a practice of living centered within the presence of the divine inner light.

Notice that the positioning of the light inner circle is directly under the centerline of the vertical axis. This is intended to symbolically express the idea taught in the Course that it is only in the present, the time we call now, when one can be within the inner alter, the circle of Atonement. It is only in the present when one can experience the holy instant and only in the present, free from the shadows of past errors, where correction, healing, and spiritual awakening take place. The present is the resting place from which we will spiritually awaken to eternity.

WORDS TO QUERY

circle of Atonement, Great Rays, inner altar, inner light, light, light within, and spark

EXCERPTS FROM THE COURSE REGARDING THE LIGHT INNER CIRCLE

The gift of the present

> Fear is not of the present, but only of the past and future, which do not exist. (T-15.I.8)

Self-centered in the right sense

> To be egocentric is to be dis-spirited, but to be Self-centered in the right sense is to be inspired or in spirit. The truly inspired are enlightened and cannot abide in darkness. (T-4.in.1)

> Peace is an attribute *in* you. You cannot find it outside. (T-2.I.5)

> *The holiness that leads us is within us, as is our home.* (T-20.II.9)

Light

> You *are* the Kingdom of Heaven, but you have let the belief in darkness enter your mind, and so you need a new light. The Holy Spirit is the radiance that you must let banish the idea of darkness. His is the glory before which dissociation falls away, and the Kingdom of Heaven breaks through into its own. (T-5.II.4)

In many only the spark remains, for the Great Rays are obscured. Yet God has kept the spark alive so that the Rays can never be completely forgotten. If you but see the little spark you will learn of the greater light, for the Rays are there unseen. Perceiving the spark will heal, but knowing the light will create. Yet in the returning the little light must be acknowledged first, for the separation was a descent from magnitude to littleness. But the spark is still as pure as the Great Light, because it is the remaining call of creation. Put all your faith in it, and God Himself will answer you. (T-10.IV.8)

The miracle worker begins by perceiving light, and translates his perception into sureness by continually extending it and accepting its acknowledgment. (T-9.V.7)

The holy circle of Atonement

Each one you see you place within the holy circle of Atonement or leave outside, judging him fit for crucifixion or for redemption. If you bring him into the circle of purity, you will rest there with him. If you leave him without, you join him there. (T-14.V.11)

Stand quietly within this circle, and attract all tortured minds to join with you in the safety of its peace and holiness. Abide with me within it, as a teacher of Atonement, not of guilt. (T-14.V.8)

CHAPTER NINE

VERTICAL AXIS
RIGHT-HAND SIDE
AND ARROW

And with Him, you will build a ladder planted in the solid rock of faith, and rising even to Heaven. Nor will you use it to ascend to Heaven alone. (T-18.V.2.)

—*A Course in Miracles*

A ladder rising from Earth to Heaven is not a new idea, but rather Christ Jesus affirming in *A Course in Miracles* what our father Jacob saw in a dream (Gen 28:10–19; John 1:51).

The symbol of the vertical axis right-hand side is a ladder with three steps. This embodies what Christ Jesus says in *A Course in Miracles*, chapter 6, under the heading "Lessons of the Holy Spirit":

1. To have, give all to all.

A Course In Miracles Cross

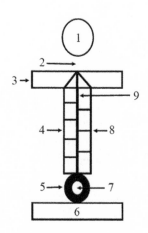

1) Circle of Creation
2) Separation
3) Longitudinal or Horizontal Plane
4) Vertical Axis Left-Hand Side
5) Dark Outer Circle
6) Foundation of Faith
7) Light Inner Circle
8) **Vertical Axis Right-Hand Side**
9) **Arrow**

2. To have peace, teach peace to learn it.
3. Be vigilant only for God and His Kingdom.

The Course refers to these three lessons as three steps. Because these steps are associated with God's plan of Atonement, spiritual awakening, and the return to the Kingdom of Heaven, they are counted from the bottom up, beginning with the first step above the base of the vertical axis, followed by the second step and then the third below the horizontal plane.

In chapter 7, *A Course in Miracles* discusses a fourth step, referred to as the last step, which is taken by God. In the symbolism of the Miracles Cross, the last step is not shown. This is because symbolically, the last step takes one from the third step of the vertical axis right-hand side, across the horizontal plane and the gap of separation to the circle of creation, which is beyond the space-time belief. The Course teaches that the last step of our journey home is one in which the separated mind is carried over from the dream of separation to reawakening to the wholeness and holiness of the Kingdom of God.

In the symbolism of the Miracles Cross, the completion of the four steps of the vertical axis right-hand side (the three steps of the ladder and the unseen last step) is associated with the complete undoing of the four steps of separation shown in the vertical axis left-hand side and thus achieving the aim of the Course, which is "removing the blocks to the awareness of love's presence, which is your natural inheritance" (T-in.7).

The vertical axis right-hand side is associated with the Holy Spirit, the Voice for God (the Healer, the Comforter, and the Guide), and His symbolic function of reinterpreting what the split mind has made in error and teaching the split mind the value of seeing in a new light. This leads to the healing of the split mind, allowing the thinker to again identify with the whole mind and to know the true Self wholly as a member of the Sonship, the family of God, within the Kingdom of God.

In the symbolism of the Miracles Cross, the vertical axis right-hand side is also associated with all things the Course teaches are right, including right-mindedness, the right answer, the right choice, the right guidance, the right learning, the right teaching, the right mind, the right perception, the right perspective, right thinking, and the right way.

The arrow in the middle of the vertical axis is centered on both the light inner circle and the longitudinal or horizontal plane and is intended to visually emphasize the importance of the aspect of time we call now, or the present. The point being that it is only by being fully present within the inner light, with no shadow of the past or anxiety for the future, in which one can ascend the ladder home to the Kingdom of Heaven. The arrow, like the ladder of the vertical axis right-hand side, is symbolic of the straight and narrow path, the path of freedom, and the path of spiritual awakening, leading us out of bondage and home again to the Kingdom of God, the Kingdom of Heaven.

WORDS TO QUERY

journey, ladder, last step, path, right, road, step, straight and vertical

EXCERPTS FROM THE COURSE REGARDING THE VERTICAL AXIS RIGHT-HAND SIDE AND THE ARROW

Correction from the bottom up

The idea of orders of need, which follows from the original error that one can be separated from God, requires correction at its own level before the error of perceiving levels at all can be corrected. You cannot behave effectively while you function on different levels. However, while you do, correction must be introduced vertically from the bottom up. This is because you think you live in space, where concepts such as "up" and "down" are meaningful. Ultimately, space is as meaningless as time. Both are merely beliefs. (T-1.VI.3)

"No man cometh unto the Father but by me" does not mean that I am in any way separate or different from you except in time, and time does not really exist. The statement is more meaningful in terms of a vertical rather than a horizontal axis. You stand below me, and I stand below God. In the process of "rising up," I am higher because without me the distance between God and man would be too great for you to encompass. I bridge the distance as an elder brother to you on the one hand, and as a Son of God on the other. My devotion to my brothers has placed me in charge of the Sonship, which I render complete because I share it. This may appear to contradict the statement "I and my Father are one," but there are two parts to the statement in recognition that the Father is greater. (T-1.II.4)

Evolution is a process in which you seem to proceed from one degree to the next. You correct your previous missteps by stepping forward. This process is actually incomprehensible in temporal terms, because you return as you go forward. (T-2.II.6)

Let us ascend in peace together to the Father, by giving Him ascendance in our minds. (T-17.IV.16)

The role of the Holy Spirit

The Holy Spirit will help you reinterpret everything that you perceive as fearful, and teach you that only what is loving is true. (T-5.IV.1)

The Holy Spirit leads you steadily along the path of freedom, teaching you how to disregard or look beyond everything that would hold you back. (T-8.II.4)

The Holy Spirit's teaching takes only *one* direction and has only *one* goal. His direction is freedom and His goal is God. (T-8.II.6)

The Holy Spirit is the Mediator between the interpretations of the ego and the knowledge of the spirit. His ability to deal with symbols enables Him to work with the ego's beliefs in its own language. His ability to look beyond symbols into eternity enables Him to understand the laws of God, for which He speaks. He can therefore perform the function of reinterpreting what the ego makes, not by destruction but by understanding. Understanding is light, and light leads to knowledge. The Holy Spirit is in light because He is in you who are light, but you yourself do not know this. It is therefore the task of the Holy Spirit to reinterpret you on behalf of God. (T-5.III.7)

The reality of now

It is evident that the Holy Spirit's perception of time is the exact opposite of the ego's. The reason is equally clear, for they perceive the goal of time as diametrically opposed. The Holy Spirit interprets time's purpose as rendering the need for time unnecessary. He regards the function of time as temporary, serving only His teaching function, which is temporary by definition. His emphasis is therefore on the only aspect of time that can extend to the infinite, for *now* is the closest approximation of eternity that this world offers. It is in the reality of "now," without past or future, that the beginning of the appreciation of eternity lies. For only "now" is here, and only "now" presents the opportunities for the holy encounters in which salvation can be found. (T-13.IV.7)

Right-mindedness

The term "right-mindedness" is properly used as the correction for "wrong-mindedness," and applies to the state of mind that induces accurate perception. It is miracle-minded because it heals misperception, and this is indeed a miracle in view of how you perceive yourself. (T-3.IV.4)

Right-mindedness listens to the Holy Spirit, forgives the

world, and through Christ's vision, sees the real world in its place. (C-1.5.2)

Crossing the bridge

Across the bridge it is so different! For a time the body is still seen, but not exclusively, as it is seen here. The little spark that holds the Great Rays within it is also visible, and this spark cannot be limited long to littleness. Once you have crossed the bridge, the value of the body is so diminished in your sight that you will see no need at all to magnify it. (T-16.VI.6)

The last step

God does not take steps, because His accomplishments are not gradual. He does not teach, because His creations are changeless. He does nothing last, because He created first and for always. It must be understood that the word "first" as applied to Him is not a time concept. He is first in the sense that He is the First in the Holy Trinity Itself. He is the Prime Creator, because He created His co-creators. Because He did, time applies neither to Him nor to what He created. The "last step" that God will take was therefore true in the beginning, is true now, and will be true forever. (T-7.I.7)

The final step will still be taken for you by God, but by the third step, the Holy Spirit has prepared you for God. He is getting you ready for the translation of *having* into *being* by the very nature of the steps you must take with Him. (T-6.V.C.5)

Beyond the body, beyond the sun and stars, past everything you see and yet somehow familiar, is an arc of golden light that stretches as you look into a great and shining circle. And all the circle fills with light before your eyes. The edges of the circle disappear, and what is in it is no longer contained at all. The light expands and covers everything, extending to infinity, forever shining and with no break or limit anywhere. Within it, everything is joined in perfect continuity. Nor is it possible to imagine that anything could be outside, for there is nowhere that this light is not. (T-21.I.8)

Where stood a cross stands now the risen Christ, and ancient scars are healed within His sight. An ancient miracle has come to bless and to replace an ancient enmity that came to kill. In gentle gratitude do God the Father and the Son return to what is Theirs, and will forever be. Now is the Holy Spirit's purpose done. For They have come! For They have come at last! (T-26. IX.8)

CHAPTER TEN

WHO WILL GO?

As a son has arisen to our Father, so too shall a
father arise to our Son, yet a father shall not ascend
alone, but with all so willing.

—*Joseph*

The following are some of the experiences this writer has
had with the Holy Spirit of God, the Voice for God, the
Universal Inspiration.

WHO WILL GO?

Be*love*d, herein rests the whole truth; blessings of peace be
with you now and with all that follows mere commentary
and recollection. "Let us not forget, however, that words are
but symbols of symbols. They are thus twice removed from
reality" (M-21.1.9).

Once upon a time, I know not when, in a place I know not
where, I heard the Voice call out, "Who will go?"

The Voice was not so much God's voice, as it was the Voice

for God (the voice representing God), in the place where I was, yet was nought.

I said nothing, wanting only to leave way for one more worthy, thinking surely there must be at least one more worthy than me to answer the call of God.

But I heard no one reply, only the echo of the Voice as it began to ebb and flow, to and fro, rhythmically across the waters of my mind. Until finally the very last wave, then the very last ripple, then the very last drop of sound was gone, leaving all in its wake perfectly still, soaking now in a sea of silence.

I then felt myself, all—alone.

This caused my mind to issue forth a sole request—that the Voice might sound again to crack open the shell of silence in which I found myself encased.

With hope, I could only listen and wait for an hour or an age, none but time can say, until again I heard the Voice ring out, "Who will go?"

Instantly I heard my heart resound, "I will."

I was not even sure that I had a heart until I heard it answer the call. And while I was glad to know I had a heart that knew our duty, I wondered what would happen next and if my heart had answered too loudly, for indeed it had answered as loudly as called.

A great angel of mercy then appeared to lead us out, and I saw away, afar afield, in the not so distant below, Mother Earth in her glory, most beautiful to behold.

Respectful of the great angel, I did not ask directly but instead said to myself, but loud enough for the great angel to overhear, "Why would I want to go there? Why would anyone want to go there?" I said this because we both knew the people on Earth had fallen asleep to a fearful dream of being separated from God.

The great angel of mercy gave me no reply but instead slowly began to raise its arms. As it did, a veil of mist, which I had not previously noticed began to lift. Revealed below I saw God's children on Earth in great distress and suffering, which I knew was *not* God's will.

As I listened, I could hear the cries of God's children rising up with the groans of Mother Earth below, all calling out for the help of God. Hearing this caused my heart to well up until it ignited a flame that continued to increase with such force and intensity that, try as I might, I could not keep contained within. And it burst forth in all directions as a great light of compassion, which shined so brightly within that nothing was left without.

It was only then that I remembered—this is why we go, this is why we leave, saying aloud so that even the four corners of the universe could hear it be said, "God's will be done!"

HEAVEN

Now, regarding hu-man being and experiences associated with coming and going, so called "a sending" and "ascending." I remember making it back to heaven and experiencing the indescribable joy marked by the occasion. I recall feeling a sense of great relief, knowing I had finally made it back.

As I approached an outer gate, many brothers and sisters rushed out to welcome me back from my sojourn. And to each of them I gave gratitude and love, and we all gave thanks to God to be together again. And it was with full certainty that I boldly declared unto them, "I will never leave this place again."

But no sooner did I say that, an elder brother, hooded like a monk such that I could not see his face, came close and whispered, "You will leave again."

Taken aback, feigning confidence while attempting to salvage any reason for my suddenly suspect statement, rather hastily I replied, "Why would I ever want to leave such a place as this?"

The elder brother then pressed to me even more closely so that only I could hear him say, "You will leave to go back for the others."

It was then that I remembered the others and that all had not yet returned. I then knew that what the elder brother had foretold would be true and that it was I who was sadly mistaken. For I thought I was in Heaven, but I was not. How could I possibly be in Heaven, knowing even one was still lost in the desert of darkness and sincerely crying out for help to make their way home again?

And so it was—I could not bear to stay in a place I had thought that I would never want to leave.

A CURRENT CARNATION

I was on the other side, being what you might call a junior staff person. We were all aware the earth was about to go through a time of passage, shifting to the new world in the new era. We also knew that the people on Earth might soon experience, on a global scale, events of their own making, which would require them to demonstrate clearly where they placed their faith: in themselves alone or in God's eternal and unconditional love for them.

My heart knew our Father's love for His children and reminded me that in their time of need I should not leave them to walk alone. I agreed and did as my heart asked me to do and told my brothers, "My heart must walk with our Father's children on Earth in their time of need, and I am willing to accept their fate as mine as well, whatever that may be, so help me God. Amen."

Theater-like, my brothers began to counsel me against it, saying my work was with them. And they said, "Even if you are allowed to leave, you will not be able to take any of your powers with you." To which I replied, "Powers or no, my heart must walk with God's children on Earth during the time of passage."

To settle my heart's request, we appealed to the court of our judge, who, by the power of wisdom and the ability to know the heart's true intent, was given charge to decide such matters in accordance with the will of our Father. I welcomed judgment, knowing my heart's intention to be true. Our judge determined the same and proclaimed so before his court and my brothers as he gave me his blessing and permission to leave.

Soon after, I overheard my soul ask another old soul if she would agree to be my mother, give birth to me on Earth, and help raise me. She had studied the way of light and love on Earth for a long time. I thought I would learn much from her, and so I felt glad, thinking that she would be my mother.

But she refused, saying she did not want to be my mother because she knew that I would be too much trouble to raise. Having already experienced all she cared to learn from raising difficult children, she said she did not want to be my mother.

I then felt humbled. And now knowing that I would be too much trouble to raise, I became discouraged, thinking no one would want to be my mother and that my heart would not be able to walk with God's children on Earth in their time of need.

I then overheard my soul ask a second, much younger soul, if she would agree to be my mother, to give birth to me on Earth, and to help raise me. Instantly, with no hesitation and filled with joy, I heard her say, "I will."

I then felt honored because although she was a young soul, having relatively little experience in the mystery of life on Earth, she was a beautifully luminous soul, with great purity of heart and of high-quality substance, even more refined than my own. I felt honored knowing that she would be my mother and that some of her substance would be used to mend and form mine. Filled with great joy, I accepted her to be my mother, to give birth to me on Earth, and to help raise me.

I was then shown different body types and allowed to choose which one I wanted. I was shown a beautiful woman with great spiritual intelligence, and I experienced in my mind's eye what it would be like to be her. But I did not like being that woman because men who knew better made fools of themselves only to try to win her favor and to bump against me. I did not like seeing men making fools of themselves, nor did

I like hearing their words of flattery, knowing they had no shame and would say anything they thought I wanted to hear. And so I chose not to be that woman. I was then shown the body I have now, and I asked if I could go like that. They said, "Yes." And so it was agreed, I would go like that.

Accompanied by a handful of angels, I was led out on high as they encircled me and began making final preparations. Then, just as I was about to go, the chief of the angels said to me softly, "You cannot take your name with you; you must leave it here with us."

Hearing this, my mind seized, unable to move, unable to comprehend the thought that was so completely...incomprehensible! I then felt all my strength begin to fly away from me as if called back to some mysterious, primal source. I then realized that my strength had never really been mine to begin with but was instead a precious gift that I now was sorry for having taken for granted. I then solemnly promised to whoever might care enough to listen that if I could be given another chance, I would never do that again. I then felt my knees buckle and my legs collapse from under me.

Feeling completely abandoned, I fell with my thoughts headfirst into the depths of chaos.

The attending ones, somehow anticipating all this, quickly closed ranks around me and held me upright.

Unable to face the unthinkable thought of leaving my name, I looked down and began to cry. But seeing that on high there is no place for tears to go, I had to quickly make for myself an abyss of sorrow so that my tears would have a place to fall.

Desperate, like a drowning man lunging for a piece of passing straw, I thought that if my tears could fill up the abyss of my despair, then perhaps I could float up upon them and make escape somewhere above, for I saw none in the deep below.

I then gave all my will to it, unleashing a vast ocean of bitter tears into the gaping hole, hoping to fill it up and make my escape. But instead, I saw the vast ocean of bitter tears fall farther and farther below, becoming smaller and smaller, until finally I saw the vast ocean of bitter tears transform into a single, tiny, insignificant, and completely meaningless teardrop, which then vanished from sight, as if swallowed down the throat of some ravenous beast lurking below.

Looking deeply into the pit of my sorry, seeing it had no bottom, and so knowing it could not be filled, I lifted my head again, and facing the thought unthinkable, I cried out to the attending ones, "If I cannot take my name with me, then I cannot go. My name was given to me by my Father; my name is who I am!"

Appealing to a sense of reason, which I could only hope they shared, pitifully I sobbed, "How will our Father know me if I don't have a name—if I don't have a name, how will I know when our Father calls for me?"

The attending ones gave me no reply, but instead they began to draw down, as if somewhere high above us was a fountain of infinite love. And ever so gently, they began to very slowly and deliberately draw down from it, pouring it over me, ministering it to me in a loving and well-coordinated manner.

Inspired by the soothing waves of relief they so sweetly washed over me, I took heart and agreed to leave my name.

Filled now with only gratitude for the love I had received in the time of my ordeal, I turned my head slightly over my right shoulder but without taking my eyes off of Mother Earth below and asked the chief angel, "At least will the ones who know, know who I am?" As somehow, I just then remembered the others, those already ahead of me, already on station, and already in labor for God's plan of Atonement. I felt completely assured, hearing the chief angel say, "They will."

THE ZIPPER

As a toddler, I remember playing on the floor with a toy one day and seeing my mother get up and leave the room. I then began to wonder if my mother still knew what I was thinking, even though she couldn't see me. Up to this time, I naturally assumed that my mother always knew what I was thinking. After all, even when I didn't say anything, she always seemed to know when I was hungry or tired. However, now at a stage all little ones go through, I found myself wondering if I was alone with my thoughts. To test the hypothesis, I decided to think something. If my mother knew what it was, she would immediately react.

On the coffee table, I noticed the lighter that my mother used for lighting incense. I had already learned that to play with the little stick that could make fire, or to even touch it, earned a, "bad, no, no, bad," followed by a few sharp slaps to the back of my hands, which hurt my pride more than anything else.

To begin my first experiment, I thought to go over and play with the lighter on the coffee table; there was no reaction from my mother in the other room. Again, I thought to go play with the lighter, but this time I made the thought louder in my mind. Again, no reaction from my mother in the other room. Then I did it a third time, this time shouting the thought to go play with the lighter as loudly as I could in my mind, but there was still no reaction from my mother in the other room. Then, as if struck by a bolt of lightning, I thought, "Oh no, what have we done?" Thinking my mother and I had somehow lost our thought connection and that I was now left alone with only my own thoughts.

Instantly, I heard a young man's voice calmly say, "It's all right. It never really happened." In my mind's eye, I was shown a zipper, like the kind you see on a pair of pants or a jacket. As I watched, one side of the zipper began to unzip while the other side began to zip back up. At the same time that the zipper had become completely unzipped, it had completely zipped back up again, all in the same moment of time. And then the zipper, now completely zipped up again, disappeared, leaving no trace, as if it had never been.

I then understood illusion and how something could seem to happen but not really happen at all, just as the young man's voice had said, and how something could be both done and undone, all at once and in the same instant.

I remember feeling glad to know that I had a mind's eye that worked. But mostly I was grateful that I wasn't alone with my thoughts. Realizing this, I felt a great surge of gratitude leap up from my heart, shooting straight up to Heaven, giving thanks to God.

I then began to wonder about whom it was that did know what I was thinking all the time. But he didn't say his name, and I did not see him. I had only heard his kind voice and saw the vision of the zipper he showed me. At first, I thought of him all the time; he was like a big brother who I knew was always with me. For a while, I felt him very close and so talked to him all the time. But then I learned that if I talked to someone who I knew was there but was invisible, it made my mother worry about me, so I stopped because my mother already had enough to worry about.

ASLEEP IN THE LIVING ROOM

The following is an account of an experience I had completely forgotten about and did not remember again until my early twenties while in solitary confinement. When I later told my mother about the experience and described where it took place, she said I was describing the apartment we lived in when I was three and four years old, on Pleasant Street in Long Beach, California.

I woke up on the couch in the living room of our small apartment and saw the test pattern on the television. A feeling of great excitement went through my body from head to toe as I realized that my little brothers and mother had all gone to bed hours earlier and that I was now up all by myself, up way past my bedtime. This was the latest I had ever been up alone.

My mother and I had been watching television earlier that evening. When she got tired and said it was time for bed, I begged her to please let me stay up to see how the movie ended. She agreed but only after I promised to turn the television off and go straight to bed after the movie was over. But instead, by accident, I fell asleep on the couch in the living room.

And now wide awake, I noticed the soft glow of a light that filled the room and my mind with great wonder. I knew something was happening, but I didn't know what. Instinctively, I sprang to my hands and knees, and now on all fours on the couch in the living room, I began looking around to see where the wondrous glow was coming from. It was disorienting because common sense told me the light should be coming from the direction of the television, which was still on, but instead the soft glow was coming from the kitchen, where the light was off.

Staring into the kitchen, I could see the enchanting light become brighter. Then I thought I saw something, or maybe it was someone, I wasn't sure, come right through the kitchen wall, joining the glowing light. But it was still too dark to clearly see, and, because the only entrance into the kitchen was the opening from the living room, I thought I must be mistaken. But then again, I saw what I saw, and so I didn't know what to think.

A few steps from the kitchen, down a short hallway, my mother and little brothers were asleep in the bedrooms. I felt my neck snap as my head turned to check the front door. I could see by the light coming from the television that the front door was closed and the bolt, which was too high for me to reach, was still on.

Panic then squeezed my chest so tight I couldn't breathe as I was struck by the thought that my family and I were now locked inside our own apartment, trapped with an intruder I thought I had seen coming right through the kitchen wall!

I knew that if my family was threatened in any way, I would have to somehow get between them and anything that might cause them harm. But I didn't know what I would do; I was just a small child.

I then saw one more, and then another, come through the wall into the kitchen to join the first one I thought I had seen come in just moments earlier. Before I wasn't sure, but now the glowing light had become so bright that I could clearly see three big people (grown-ups) standing together in the kitchen with the glowing light. I could hardly believe what I saw.

As I watched, theater-like, I saw the three beings in the kitchen begin making a commotion, opening the silverware drawer and rattling the forks, spoons, and knives, as if they were about to steal something. But I didn't see them take anything. I couldn't help but wonder, why are they here, and what do they want?

Crouching on the couch in the living room, wound tight as a kitten ready to pounce, I watched as the three, now moving together as one, began to slowly float out of the kitchen and into the living room, as if they were following the glowing light.

Seeing all this, my mind filled with terrible thoughts. I suddenly realized that all the tenseness in my body that was ready for action had changed; in an unguarded moment, I had become frozen stiff with fear. I couldn't move a muscle, no matter how hard I tried. Instead, the only movement I was able to make was an involuntary and painful one. It was my heart, beating wildly with the force of a sledgehammer. I had no doubt that I was about to die. I thought that either the force of my pounding heart would cause my chest to crack wide open, or, because my heart was pounding so loudly, that it would give me away. Either way, I thought for sure I would soon be dead.

I thought to myself, if I am about to die, I must be brave and die without making a sound. I knew that if my mother heard me cry out, she would wake up and come to see what was wrong. And then they might hurt her too. With both of us gone, there would be no one left to take care of my little brothers.

Thus, to my fear of dying was added a much more dreadful thought—that I might not be brave enough to die without making a sound. Maybe I was a coward; I didn't know. In a single instant, all these fearful thoughts pierced my brain like a barrage of rusty iron arrows.

As I watched the three, moving as one, silently floating out of the kitchen, I felt a sense of relief at seeing that they did not turn down the hallway toward the bedrooms where my family was sleeping. But in the next instant, the feeling of relief changed to complete terror, as I saw them coming straight toward me, as if they knew I had been there the whole time—a little boy hiding on the other side of the couch, spying on them from the shadows in the living room.

The three floated into the living room and stopped right in front of me. My full attention went to the one in front who led them. It was a great lady full of grace, most beautiful to behold.

Our eyes met, and as they did, all my fear vanished, as if it had never been. I could see in the great lady's eyes that she loved me, and I, too, felt a great love for her. I thought that maybe when I got big I would marry her, while at the same time wondering why in the world would she ever want to marry me?

And with all fear now gone, I could see that the enchanting light, which I had first noticed when I woke up, was actually her light and that she herself was composed of luminous light. She had fashioned her light into a glorious gown of light, which shone brightly all around her.

With the great lady full of grace were two men who seemed to be both her friends and her escorts. The great lady introduced herself and her companions, but I have forgotten their names. On the right-hand side of the great lady was a young man with no beard and golden-brown hair. When I looked into his eyes, I could see that he, too, loved me, and I felt a deep love for him. It was as if we were family, but I didn't know how we could possibly be related. Standing on the left-hand side of the great lady was a very old man with a long beard. When I looked into his eyes, I saw that he was most ancient.

I quickly looked back to the great lady full of grace, and with her eyes, she gave me permission to take their full measure, which I did. Most striking was the great lady, wearing her glorious gown of luminous light. She was so beautiful to behold that it was not easy to look away from her. But with some effort, I was able to look down and saw her feet and those of her companions. I saw that their feet were bare and that they had no shoes. I felt pity for them, thinking they must be poor people, like the ones my mother taught me to pray for, who had come not to steal anything but were looking for shoes because they had none.

With my eyes, I told the great lady I was very sorry, but I had no shoes to give them. The great lady was taller than my mother, and I didn't know of any men's shoes in the house, only little boy shoes, which were too small.

The ancient one then seemed to become upset with me because I had pitied them for being poor and having no shoes. With his eyes, I heard him gruffly ask the great lady, "Why are we wasting time with this one?" I then felt humbled and embarrassed, as I had intended no offense. The great lady then made a gesture with her hand, so subtly that it was almost invisible, which gently asked the ancient one to hold his peace. And he did.

The young man then used his eyes to tell me to follow him. Eagerly, I climbed off the couch to go with him. He then put me in a vision where I was locked in a room alone. A criminal came into the room with me, so I became a little afraid. The room then began to fill up with more and more bad men, and as it did, I became more and more afraid.

I thought there must be some mistake. I had not done anything wrong; I was just a child who had stayed up too late watching television and had not gone to bed when I was supposed to, as I had promised. Instead, by mistake, I had accidently fallen asleep on the couch in the living room. So I thought it was a mistake and wrong that I should be locked in a room crowded with bad men.

I then heard the voice of the young man ask me, "Do you want to be there?"

I shouted back, "No!"

He said, "Then be good." Immediately I was taken out of the vision and was standing beside the young man again. I then thought to myself, my mother is right—I really should try harder to be good.

The young man then showed me a vision. Together we watched as a corner of the ceiling opened up and high above a great and mighty angel of God came out, who I knew was going out to do God's will. It was a glorious sight to behold.

After the great and mighty angel of God had gone from sight, we continued to watch together. A second great and mighty angel of God then came out from on high, again like the first one had done, also going out to do God's will.

As we watched the second great angel go out of sight, my mind became confused. I couldn't imagine what it could be that would require a second great and mighty angel of God to have to leave Heaven because I knew most certainly the first one had more than enough power to carry out God's will.

Sensing my confusion, the young man used his mind to tell my mind that there is a great battle going on. But the angels of God are not allowed to use all their power, and that is why a second was sent; the first had done all it rightfully could under God's law. But the battle continued, so a second was sent.

As the young man and I continued to watch together, a third great, mighty angel of God came out from on high, again like the others, going out to do God's will. Seeing this, my heart filled with love for God's will so strongly that, without thinking, I turned my head, looked up into the young man's eyes, and pointing to the angel above, blurted out, "I want to be like them!"

The young man subtly laughed to himself and said, mostly to himself it seemed, "Maybe one day?" But because of his sublime subtlety, I was unable to tell if he was laughing at me for having such a foolish idea, an idea that only a small child could even imagine. Or maybe he knew something I didn't. I dared not ask and instead chose to safely assume my heart's desire was a foolish one.

The young man then led me a short way. We stopped to wait briefly. Then a supremely noble great man approached us. He was very tall, with dark hair and a beard, wearing polished riding boots. He walked toward us with all the bearing and authority of a high commander, a supremely noble servant of God's will.

I could not even imagine how I could be worthy enough to be in his presence.

The young man introduced us. The supremely noble one and I conversed. He asked me a few questions to which my heart responded. He then showed me the people on Earth going about their daily life. As we watched together, we could feel the drudgery and despair of their daily existence. The great servant of God's will then asked me what I thought the people needed most. I thought they needed a great many things, but unable to decide on just one thing and wanting to be honest but not wanting to misspeak, I replied, "I don't know what the people need most."

The great servant of God's will then asked me if I thought the people needed God's love the most. Immediately I replied yes, realizing right away it was really *all* the people needed. The great servant of God's will then asked me if I would help him to help the people. I said yes but quickly added that I did not think that anyone would listen to me because I was just a little boy. No one would think I knew anything. The supremely noble one told me not to worry about it, saying he would take care of that part.

He then offered to be my teacher. Overjoyed and filled with a sense of great gratitude and humility, I agreed to be one of his pupils. At the conclusion of our meeting, he gave me permission to look deeply into his eyes, and I did so. His eyes were the color of pure potential energy, an infinite see of unlimited power and possibility. He then turned his eyes away after the smallest of moments, saying, "That is enough." He had turned away just in the nick of time—I could have vanished blissfully into his eyes without a second thought.

My teacher then led me to the doorway of another room, where about ten people were standing outside in the hallway. They were all wearing their costumes (the clothes they wore when they were alive on Earth). They were famous artists of sounds, colors, and letters, who had lived in the past, giving their labor of love to bring beauty and culture to humanity on Earth. One appeared to even have been a queen. We all seemed to be connected but in a way that I did not understand.

My teacher then led me around, introducing me to everyone. We greeted each other formally yet in a warm and friendly manner. We all went into the room together, then entered a larger domed chamber. It was a little strange because I felt as if I was still in our apartment, but at the same time, I felt like I was in a different place. I simply reasoned that space must have different levels sharing the same place, like different layers of a layer cake all share the same cake.

As we entered the large domed chamber, I saw in the middle of the room a column of fire blazing up from the floor. It was a few feet taller than me. As we approached, the notables encircled me. I now stood alone, facing the towering flame.

I could feel the ring of notables' silent encouragement for me to enter into the fire. But I was frightened, thinking that I would be burned alive and die. So, I stood there, too afraid to move, not knowing what else to do. This caused the ring of notables to gently increase their silent encouragement. As they did, I turned my head to look at those around me and saw my teacher. Looking into his eyes, I remembered my vow, his promise, and our cause. Leaving all fear behind, I stepped into the middle of the column of fire, seeing only the fire surrounding me.

To my complete surprise, I was not burned alive, nor did I feel discomfort of any kind. I was filled with thankfulness to still be alive. I then felt myself being lifted. As if some invisible force, like a magnet, was gently lifting me up into the mind of God.

I felt relieved when the ascent stopped because although reason told me I had not gone all the way up, I had gone up as far as I dared to go. I thought it would not have been right for me to go any farther.

Then I saw before me a beautiful crystal-clear mountain lake. Around the lake were pine trees and snowcapped mountain peaks. As I observed all this, I became aware that I had the consciousness of the entire scene; I was all that I beheld, and all that I beheld was me. There was no separation in between. I was the snowcapped mountain peaks; I was the pine trees; and I was the beautiful crystal-clear mountain lake.

I then became aware that I could easily move my awareness as I willed. I then directed my focus on the bed of sand at the bottom of the crystal-clear mountain lake, directing my mind to behold a single grain of sand. To my astonishment, the joyous feeling did not change in any way. I realized there was as much beauty and joy to be found in a single grain of sand as there was to be experienced by being the entire crystal-clear mountain lake scene.

As the multitude of the grains of sand and the beauty that was everywhere began to dawn on me, I felt my consciousness pulse out in waves as if a pebble of insight had been dropped into a perfectly still pool of being, releasing ever-expanding spheres of conscious cosmic beingness.

The next thing I remember was lying again on the couch in the living room where I had earlier fallen asleep while watching television. The great lady full of grace then used her eyes to call me out of my body. I came out easily and followed her and her two companions as they floated up and out through the wall in the living room.

I floated along behind them but stopped when I came to the wall. Surely, I thought, I can't fly through the wall as they had done. The great lady then called to me from the other side of the wall to join them. But I told her I couldn't because the wall blocked the way. Then in a motherly tone that I knew meant business, I heard her say, "Come here now!" Immediately I moved out of my fear, surprised by how easily I went through the wall, as if it wasn't even there. I then joined the great lady who was by herself on the other side.

As we began going down a path together, I was struck by how flat it was—a flatness that could be felt.

I knew I was walking with the great lady full of power and grace and promised myself that while I was with her, I would stay on my very best behavior. And I had no doubt in my mind that I would be able to do so.

As we went along the path together, I noticed to our right nothing of interest, but to the left of the path was a row of green hedges, several feet high and a few feet deep.

After we had traveled a short way, we stopped. The great lady looked at me, and with her eyes, she said, "Wait." Then she was gone from sight, leaving me alone on the path.

I waited for a little while until I noticed on the other side of the hedges were two children playing in a field. I wanted to go and play with them, to make friends, and to let them know they were not alone. That I was there with them too.

Determined to make friends with the children, I began trying to wriggle my way through the hedges. But after much effort, I became exhausted and was not even halfway through. Suddenly, the branches came alive. Snakelike, they began wrapping themselves around my wrists and ankles. And as they held me taut, another snakelike branch wrapped itself around my neck, as if to strangle me. I used all my strength to try to get away, but it was no use.

Realizing I had come to my last breath and was facing

death, without thinking, I called out in my mind so loudly as to be heard from one end to the other, "Father!"

Immediately I heard the Voice calmly reply, "Use your mind."

I then felt humbled. Despite my grave situation, I was not going to be divinely rescued and instead only given guidance as to what *I* needed to do to save myself.

Feeling the grip on my very last breath slipping away and having no time to feel in the least bit slighted, I used my mind and willed the hedges to release me, which they immediately did.

As I landed softly on the ground, scrambling away without a scratch, I thought to myself, "People do have power over nature, but we just don't believe it." And now safely out of danger, I forgot all about the hedges and the Voice as I walked over to make friends and play with the other children.

Getting closer, I could see the two children playing in the field appeared to be brother and sister. The girl appeared to be a little older. I went up to them and tried to make friends and play. But they were not the least bit interested, acting as if they didn't care if I was there or not. And in a strange way, they didn't seem to be real at all.

As I turned to go, I saw the great lady full of grace standing beside me. And as soon as I saw her, I remembered what she had told me to do: wait. But somehow, by mistake, I had forgotten. Words cannot describe how upset I was with myself or how ashamed I felt.

As the great lady and I left the field together, taking the path back in the direction we had come, I carried a heavy burden. It was my heart, crushed by the weight of sadness and deepest regret for what I had done. I did not fear the great lady's power, nor was I concerned at all with any punishment. I knew she would not harm me in any way. Rather, I felt horrible because I loved her and knew she loved me and that she had asked me to do only one thing—wait. But instead, I had forgotten and had used all my strength to disobey her.

Unable to carry the burden of my monumental regret any farther, I stopped, and somehow finding the strength to look into the eyes of the great lady, I told her with my eyes and all my heart that I was truly sorry.

With her eyes, she told me I was forgiven.

My heart jumped with joy, like a colt turned to pasture, innocent and free again. And I was surprised because, while I thought I loved the great lady as much as I could, when she forgave me, I felt my love for her increase. I did not think it was possible but was glad it was so.

Effortlessly, we floated back together through the wall and into the living room, where I saw my body sleeping on the couch. I didn't want to go back into my body, but I was drawn in, as if sucked in by a powerful magnet. Reentering my body felt like a jail door being slammed closed. I felt imprisoned and became very depressed. But then I became aware of a silvery thread of light with life, which was connected to my heart. Knowing that my heart was connected to a thread of light with life was the only thing that made being back in my body tolerable because it gave me hope that my entrapment would be temporary.

Sensing that the great lady full of grace and her two companions were preparing to leave, I woke myself up and climbed off the couch to go with them. But they said I couldn't go with them now; I had to wait. I stopped dead in my tracks and began to cry.

The young man then came back to where I was. He looked deeply into my eyes, and, with his eyes, he told me to follow him. I then began to follow his eyes to see where he was looking as he looked deeper and deeper into my eyes.

In his eyes, I saw great love for what he saw and thought he loved me because I was special. But then I noticed that he was looking through me, past all the layers of me, to something deeper within.

I then felt a little embarrassed for thinking he loved me because I was special, while at the same time feeling relieved I wasn't. I felt glad to know that I was just a regular person, like anyone else.

As I continued to look into the young man's eyes, following where they led, I then saw what he was giving his love to. It was not to me but to a light within me I was not previously aware of. But now, having followed his vision all the way through me, past all the layers of me, encountering this light, I, too, became filled with a profound love and reverence for the light within.

I then offered the light that was in me to the young man, knowing he was worthier than I to carry such a glorious light. He gracefully declined and revealed to me the light within him, which was the same as the light in me. We shared a wonderful moment together, loving the light of

God and giving our thanks to God that it was in both of us. He then returned to his friends, who were patiently waiting for him.

Seeing the three rise up as one and begin to float out of the living room, I could not help myself and again begged the great lady full of grace to please let me come with them. But she said, "You must wait." They then floated through the wall and were gone.

I did not move from the spot where I saw them last. I lay down right there on the floor, basking in the glow of light they had kindly left behind until it blended into the first light of a new day dawning.

BLESSING THE EARTH AND PRAISING GOD

When I was about eight or nine years old, we moved to a duplex at the end of a cul-de-sac close to a small clearing with a big tree, providing plenty of shade and a cool place to play when it got too hot to play under the blazing southern California sun.

I will never forget the one day, while playing under the big tree, off in the distance I faintly heard what sounded like men chanting. As I stopped to listen, the singing became louder. Looking in the direction where the sound was coming from, I saw a group of men, maybe ten or fifteen, dressed like monks, walking in a slow, steady pace toward the big tree.

As they came closer, I couldn't believe my eyes. They were in spirit form, invisible, but somehow I could see them. It seemed as though their chanting was their way of blessing the earth and praising God all at the same time. As they walked past me, I could see they were focused on their task in a sublimely peaceful way and were unconcerned about me watching them. But after they had all passed by, I did see one of the younger ones, in the rear of the procession, turn his head around to look at me. For an instant, we made eye contact, but he just as quickly turned back around, continuing on with his brothers.

For several days after that, I went back to the big tree in the hopes of seeing them again, but I never did. And I never told anyone about what happened because I was afraid of what people might think about me. Plus, I didn't want my mother to be worried about me.

FOUNTAIN OF LIGHT WITH LIFE

In the 1990s, as a grown man, I was driving when I heard the Voice say, "Turn here." I turned quickly into a somewhat hidden driveway, leading to what I later learned was the Princeton Friends Meeting House. It was closed, but on the porch in a display case, I saw information about something called the Surrender Group. I took a pamphlet, which said the group met one night a week and was open to the general public. I wasn't a Quaker or member of any spiritual or religious group, but at that point in my life, I was aware that I needed to surrender my will to something higher and truer than my ego, which I knew was of my own making.

I began regularly attending these Surrender Group meetings, which were always insightful and most ably led by a sage named Herrymon Maurer, who never tired of reminding us of the importance of being "fully present" (here now).

At one meeting, we agreed to study the Tao Te Ching. That weekend, I went to the bookstore, purchased a copy of the Tao, returned home, and began reading in preparation for our next meeting.

I soon came to the section in which the nature of the Tao was explored. In essence, I understood the text to say that the Tao is nameless, beyond description, and ineffable. In particular, the phrase describing the nature of the Tao as "darkness within darkness" caught my attention. I wanted to know what that meant. I was pretty sure I knew what darkness was, but darkness within darkness was a new concept. I wanted to understand it...if I could.

As I thought about the phrase describing the Tao as darkness within darkness, I was reminded of the part in the Bible where the dear one says, "Ask and ye shall receive." So I decided to ask, "What, if anything, does the darkness within darkness mean?" I then also remembered the part in the Bible where the elder brother says that sometimes it is best to pray in private so that only our Father knows. And even though I was home alone, not expecting anyone anytime soon, I still felt moved to take out all the clothes, shoes, and boxes in my bedroom closet. I went inside, sat on the floor, and, pulling the door closed behind me, began to meditate on the phrase, darkness within darkness.

I soon realized that symbolically, albeit unintentionally, I was expressing and experiencing the question; sitting on the closet floor in the dark with my eyes closed, I felt like I was seeing the darkness within darkness that was indeed dark. "But what does it mean?" I asked.

After a few minutes, in my mind's eye I was taken up by an angel. Together we ascended, leaving the earth far behind. As I followed the angel upward, we went far into outer space, traveling together past all stars and constellations. We continued on past everything. I began to wonder why we continued, as it seemed to me that everything that was, was already behind us. And I confess that for a split second a feeling of doubt passed through me. I wondered if maybe the angel had lost its way. But out of respect, I dared not ask and chose instead to trust and have faith.

Then I saw before us a huge rainbow-colored fountain of light with life. It was shaped like a tube, lying horizontally. The left end was narrow, but as it continued to the right, it became larger in circumference, opening wide at the end like a cornucopia or a trumpet or a flower in full bloom.

The fountain of light with life was composed of rings of color that were all bound together, side by side in a row. Each of the vivid rings was a different color of the rainbow, with each ring having dominion of its particular sphere of color. But reason told me there must be a higher authority with sovereignty over all of the rings of color because they all fit together in perfect harmony with one another.

The left end of the fountain of light with life was connected to nothing (no thing, thus no name); however, it is more accurate to say the left end was connected to the vast infinite potential for any, every, and all things, while the right end was connected to the universe of everything that has a name.

The fountain of light with life appeared as a portal, connecting the way by which potential becomes actual, infinite becomes finite, and the nameless becomes named. Most glorious to behold was the color of each ring, brilliantly luminescent and alive with color, filled with light and life. But it was not like looking at something that was colored this color or that color; rather it was like seeing the source of color itself. As if the red ring was the source of all reds, the green ring the source of all of greens, the blue ring the source of all blues, and so on. I stood in complete amazement of what I saw.

As the angel and I watched together, out of the right end of the fountain of light with life, we saw issue forth and out into the universe of things with names a new Earth, purified and clean. As the new Earth emerged, it floated ahead of us a little farther along the way than we had traveled.

As the angel and I watched together, we next saw the fountain of light with life issue forth and out into the universe of things with names an elephant, which followed along the same way the new Earth had gone.

As the angel and I watched together, we next saw the fountain of light with life issue forth and out into the universe of things with names a newborn human baby, which followed along the same way the elephant and the new Earth had gone.

Upon seeing the baby emerge from the rainbow-colored fountain of light with life, I became awestruck and began saying aloud, over and over again, like a needle stuck on a record, "How loving, how loving, how loving," until finally I was able to garner just enough thought to ask the angel that we depart, which we did, I doing so without turning my back, in all reverence and humility for what I had been shown.

CENTER YOURSELF

As an adult, I was in a spiritual chat room on the internet in the mid-1990s. Someone who I had just met said he felt like he was being guided to tell me something, but he said he didn't know how to say it. I suggested he speak as the Spirit moved him. A few minutes later, he sent back the following. I don't know who he was, and I don't remember his name. And this was our only communication.

Center yourself upon the reality of God
Aware of its dependability to cleanse and to prime your truth-seeking mind
For the spiritual journey along your path
At your core you are part of the absolute
Surrounded by the total effects of the experience garnered in former lives
Which signify the duration of time required for the realization of your divinity
Determine your thoughts shall unfailingly mirror the light of your Godly heritage

ABOUT THE AUTHOR

The oldest of four boys, Joseph was born in Long Beach, California, in 1955. His often-absent father was sentenced to prison when Joseph was seven years old. A few years later, his mother married a man who frequently physically abused him. The family moved often, and while growing up, Joseph attended ten different schools in six different states: California, Louisiana, Arkansas, Missouri, Pennsylvania, and New Jersey. At the age of thirteen, living in Philadelphia, Pennsylvania, where his street name was White Hawk, Joseph was a chronic truant from school and a runaway from home. Once he even hitchhiked to New York City; another time he hopped a freight train to Baltimore, Maryland. While living in southern New Jersey, Joseph dropped out of high school and, after getting into trouble with the law, joined the army, where he obtained his high school equivalency diploma, served for four years, and was an arctic paratrooper stationed in Alaska. Using the GI Bill, Joseph graduated from the College of New Jersey, where he majored in philosophy and was an honors student. He later received a Master of Social Work from Rutgers, the State University of New Jersey. Joseph currently works full-time as a social worker in the field of child protection, a career he began in 1997 as an investigator of child abuse and neglect allegations. Joseph and his wife married in 1983. They live in South Brunswick, New Jersey, and have one child, who is now an adult. Joseph is a Christian but not affiliated with any particular denomination or church. He has been a student of *A Course in Miracles* since 1996.

Author website: www.acourseinmiraclescross.org
Author email: Joseph@acourseinmiraclescross.org